Teach Your Cat

GUERNESIAIS

Teach Your Cat

GUERNESIAIS

Anne Cakebread

y Lolfa

Thank you to:
Helen, Marcie, Lily and Nina, my family, friends and neighbours in St Dogmaels for all their support and encouragement, the States of Guernsey,
Josephine Dowding, Carolyn at Y Lolfa and Yan Marquis for Guernesiais translations and pronunciations.
Merci bian.

In memory of Frieda, who started us on the
Teach Your Dog journey.

First impression: 2022

© Anne Cakebread & Y Lolfa Cyf., 2022

Illustrations and design by Anne Cakebread

ISBN: 978-1-80099-202-3

Published and printed in Wales on paper from well-maintained forests by Y Lolfa Cyf., Talybont, Ceredigion SY24 5HE
e-mail ylolfa@ylolfa.com
website www.ylolfa.com
tel 01970 832 304
fax 832 782

*Guernesiais has no universally agreed spelling or grammar.
The translator has aimed to reflect usage and may have
employed stylistic choices. At times there is no exact expression
in the target language, so an equivalent might be used.
No liability is assumed by the translator.*

I grew up only speaking English.
When I moved to west Wales, I adopted Frieda,
a rescue whippet, who would only obey
Welsh commands.
Slowly, whilst dealing with Frieda, I realised that I was
overcoming my nerves about speaking Welsh aloud, and
my Welsh was improving as a result – this gave me the
idea of creating a series of books to help others learn.
You don't even have to go abroad to practise.
If you haven't got a cat, any pet or soft toy
will do: just have fun learning and speaking
a new language.

– Anne Cakebread

"Hello"

"Ouâroh"

pron:

"Worr<u>ow</u>"

stress
this

"Come here"

"Vians ichin"

pron:

"V'y<u>o</u> eesha-ee"

'o'
as in
'h<u>o</u>t'

"Leave it!"

"Lâque-lé!"

pron:
"Lark-l̲e̲!"

'e'
as in
'm̲e̲t'

"Stop!"

"Arraête!"

pron:
"Are-rate!"

"No!"

"Nou-fait!"

pron:

"Noo-fe̲!"

'e'
as in
'me̲t'

"Very good"

"Vlà qui vaot"

pron:

"Vlo key vow"

'o'
as in
'hot'

"How much is it?"

"Coumian qu'ch'est?"

pron:

"Kom-y<u>ou</u>k-shay?"

'ou'
as in
'w<u>ou</u>ld'

"Don't scratch"

"N'lé graeme pas"

pron:
"N'l_e_ gra-eem par"

'e'
as in
'm_e_t'

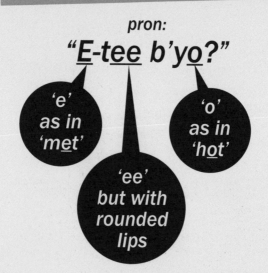

"Bedtime"

"Pour la jucque"

pron:

"Poor lo zheek"

roll the 'r' slightly

'o' as in 'hot'

'zh' as in 'Zhivago'

'ee' but with rounded lips

"Good night"

"Bouanne gniet"

pron:
"Bworn n'ye"

'e' as in 'met'

"Be quiet!"

"Tai-té!"

pron:

"Te-te!"

'e'
as in
'met'

"Wake up!"

"Éville-té!"

pron:

"**Eveel-te!**"

'e'
as in
'met'

"What's the time?"

"Quaïe haeure qu'il est?"

pron:

"Kigh a-ear keel ay?"

'igh' as in 'high'

'a' as in 'man'

pronounce the 'r'

'ay' as in 'say'

"Lunchtime"

"Dênaï"

pron:
"Day-nigh"

"Are you full?"

"As-tu assaï maugi?"

pron:

"Are-t<u>ee</u> <u>o</u>-sigh m<u>ou</u>-<u>zh</u>ee?"

'ee' but with rounded lips

'o' as in 'h<u>o</u>t'

'ou' as in 'w<u>ou</u>ld'

'zh' as in '<u>Zh</u>ivago'

"All gone"

"Tout parti"

pron:

"Too par-tee"

pronounce the 'r'

"What are you doing?"

"Tchi qu't'es à faire?"

pron:

"Cheek-tay o fair?"

'o' as in 'hot'

pronounce the 'r'

"It's snowing"

"I tcheit d'la neis"

pron:
"Ee ched l<u>o</u> nay"

'o'
as in
'h<u>o</u>t'

"It's cold"

"I fait fré"

pron:

"Ee fe fre"

'e' as in 'met'

roll the 'r' slightly

'e' as in 'met'

"It's hot"

"I fait reide caod"

pron:
*"Ee f**e** r**e**d cow"*

'e'
as in
'm**e**t'

*longer
than
normal*

"It's raining"

"I plleut"

pron:
"Ee p'ya"

'a'
as in
'ago'

"It's windy"

"I vente"

pron:
"Ee vot"

"It's a nice day"

"I fait bael"

pron:

"Ee fe bal"

'e'
as in
'met'

'a'
as in
'man'

"Come down!"

"Dvâle!"

pron:
"D'varl!"

"Do you want to play?"

"Veurs-tu jouaï?"

pron:

"Ver-tee zh-why?"

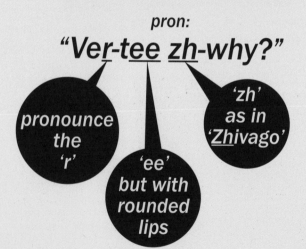

pronounce the 'r'

'ee' but with rounded lips

'zh' as in 'Zhivago'

"What have you got?"

"Tchi qu't'as?"

pron:
"Cheek-tar?"

“Where are you going?”

“Éiou qu’tu t’en vas?”

pron:

“Eyouk-tee tor var?”

‘ou’ as in ‘would’

‘ee’ but with rounded lips

"What have you been doing?"

"Tchi qu't'as fait?"

pron:

"Cheek-tar f<u>e</u>?"

'e' as in 'm<u>e</u>t'

"Have you got
a headache?"

"As-tu ma
à la taête?"

pron:

"Are-tee mala ta-eet?"

'ee'
but with
rounded
lips

"Have you got tummy ache?"

"As-tu ma dans l'corps?"

pron:

"Are-t<u>ee</u> ma dorl ko<u>r</u>?"

'ee' but with rounded lips

pronounce the 'r'

"Have you got a cold?"

"As-tu aen fré?"

pron:

"Are-t<u>ee</u> <u>a</u> fr<u>e</u>?"

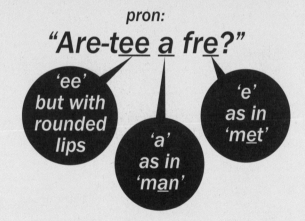

'ee'
but with
rounded
lips

'a'
as in
'm<u>a</u>n'

'e'
as in
'm<u>e</u>t'

"Where are you?"

"Éiou qu't'es?"

pron:

"Eyouk-tay?"

'ou'
as in
'would'

"Don't be afraid"

"N'seis pas gênaï"

pron:
"S<u>e</u> par <u>zh</u>ee-nigh"

'e'
as in
'm<u>e</u>t'

'zh'
as in
'<u>Zh</u>ivago'

"Get out!"

"Rence-té!"

pron:

"Rorss-t<u>e</u>!"

'e'
as in
'm<u>e</u>t'

"Is that your favourite toy?"

"Eche là ta jouaette favorite?"

'o' as in 'hot'

pron:

"Esh lo tar zhwat far-vor-reet?"

'zh' as in 'Zhivago'

"Do you
want a cuddle?"

**"Veurs-tu
aen codeul?"**

pron:

"Ver-tee a cod-earl?"

pronounce
the
'r'

'ee'
but with
rounded
lips

'a'
as in
'man'

"Cheers!"

"Sàntaï!"

pron:

"S<u>a</u>d-tie!"

longer
than
normal

"I love you"

"J't'oïme"

pron:
"Sh'toym"

"Happy Birthday"

"Bouan Jour d'Naissànce"

pron:

"Bwo zhoord-nay-sass"

'o' as in 'hot'

'zh' as in 'Zhivago'

longer than normal

"Good luck"

"Bouanne chànce"

pron:

"Bworn shass"

'a'
as in
'man',
but longer

"Merry Christmas"

"Bouan Noué"

pron:

"Bwo Nwe"

'o'
as in
'hot'

'e'
as in
'met'

"Happy New Year"

"Bouanne Aunaïe"

pron:
"Bworn On-eye"

"Thank you"

"Merci bian"

pron:

"Mer-see b'yo"

pronounce the 'r'

'o' as in 'hot'

"How many?"

"Coumian?"

pron:

"Kom-yo̲?"

'o'
as in
'ho̲t'

1
one
"ieune"

pron:
"y<u>a</u>n"

'a'
as in
'<u>a</u>go'

2
two
"daeus"

pron:
"da-ee"

3
three
"treis"

pron:
"tray"

4
four

"quate"

pron:
"cot"

5
five
"chin"

pron:
"sha-ee"

6
six
"six"

pron:
"see"

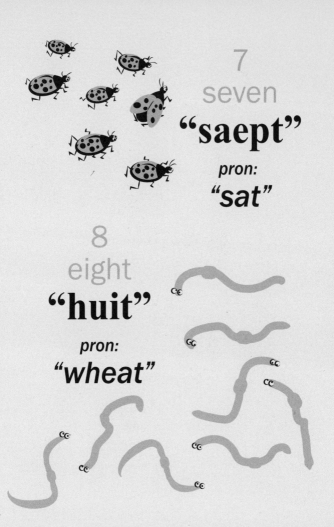

9
nine

"**neuf**"

pron:
"*nerf*"

10 ten

"dix"

pron:
"dee"

20
twenty
"**vingt**"

pron:
"va-ee"

"Are you happy?"

"Es-tu fiaer?"

pron:

"E-tee fyar?"

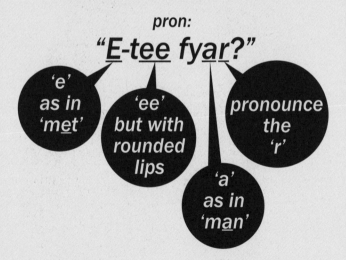

'e'
as in
'm<u>e</u>t'

'ee'
but with
rounded
lips

'a'
as in
'm<u>a</u>n'

pronounce
the
'r'

"Have you got enough room?"

"As-tu du reun assaï?"

pron:

"Are-t<u>ee</u> d<u>ee</u> r<u>ur</u> are-sigh?"

'ee' but with rounded lips

'ur' as in 'f<u>ur</u>'

"Goodbye"

"És aotes jours"

pron:

"Eez ode <u>zh</u>oor"

'zh'
as in
'<u>Zh</u>ivago'

Titles in this series include:

Teach Your Dog Cornish
Teach Your Dog French
Teach Your Dog Gaelic
Teach Your Dog Gog: North Wales Welsh
Teach your Dog Irish
Teach your Dog Italian
Teach Your Dog Japanese
(Rugby World Cup Travel Edition)
Teach Your Dog Korean
(e-book only)
Teach Your Cat Manx
Teach Your Dog Māori
Teach Your Dog Spanish
Teach Your Cat Welsh
Teach Your Dog Welsh

More coming soon!